D1432477

STICKY FACTS
WHAT WILL YOU FIND?

Animals

Welcome to your Sticky Facts activity book!

Inside are **hundreds of stickers** of creatures and critters from all over the world. From the glowing organs of an anglerfish to the number of whiskers on a walrus, we've included the wildest animal facts around.

But this is a sticker book unlike any other! In fact, as you learn about animals of the rainforest, the Arctic, and everywhere in between, you can sticker, draw, and add your own ideas to the activity pages. By the end, you'll make a book all your own that you can cherish forever.

LET'S GO EXPLORING! ➡

animal adventure!

My Explorer's Journal

Name: _____

On this journey, we'll visit:

a tundra

a desert

a savanna

an ocean

a rainforest

a coniferous forest

I want to visit the _____ first!

The animal I most want to see is _____.

Scientists estimate there are 8 to 10 million species that live on Earth! If you could see 1,000 animals a day, it would still take you more than 21 years to see them all. And new species are being discovered all the time!

ocean!

A **food chain** is the way energy is transferred from one living thing to another. Ocean animals and plants are part of food chains, which means that they depend on one another as food!

Use stickers to complete each food chain.

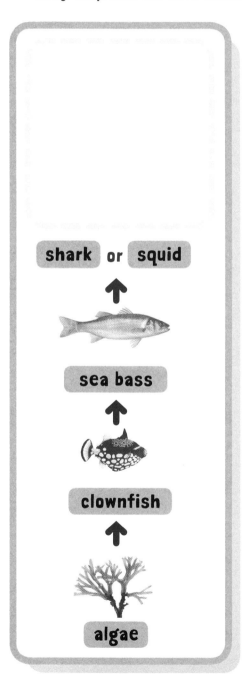

shark **or** squid

↑

sea bass

↑

clownfish

↑

algae

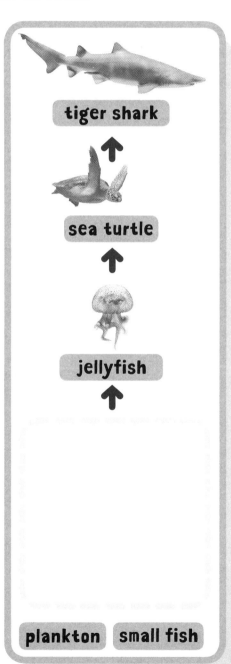

tiger shark

↑

sea turtle

↑

jellyfish

↑

plankton small fish

thresher shark

↑

tuna

↑

small fish

↑

plankton

Plankton are very tiny organisms that float in the ocean. They can be animals, called "zooplankton," or plants, called "phytoplankton."

life in the ocean

Coral reefs are technically animals, but they look a lot like plants. They attach to rocks on the ocean floor and grow in lots of different shapes and colors. Pollution and warming ocean waters threaten coral reefs. This is a big problem, because roughly 25 percent of all ocean species depend on reefs for food and shelter!

Sticker over the items that don't belong in the coral reef. Draw animals and plants that do belong in the coral reef.

savanna!

Animals use **camouflage** to hide in plain sight. In the savanna, animals blend into the grasses, rocks, and trees to avoid predators and find food.

Color the savanna terrain. Then sticker and draw animals hiding in each place.

secrets of the savanna

Sticker and draw parents for the baby animals.

Baby zebras are called "foals." When they are born, their stripes are brown and white, and they can walk within 20 minutes. Within an hour, they can run!

Ostrich eggs are bigger than your hand! The babies, which are about a foot tall at birth, are called "chicks."

Baby crocodiles are called "hatchlings." They have a special tooth to help them break out of their eggs!

tundra!

In an arctic tundra, animals make homes in the snow and icy waters!

Sticker and draw animals in their arctic tundra homes.

Snowy owls scrape out nests in the frozen ground to lay their eggs.

A polar bear's den can be about 40 degrees Fahrenheit inside even when it's below freezing outside!

Harp seals can sleep on land or in the water!

Arctic foxes often reuse other foxes'—or even squirrels'—dens that lie deep underground.

life on the ice

How do animals stay warm in the icy water? They have a thick layer of fat called **blubber**! The blubber helps to keep the cold temperatures out and the warm body heat inside.

Sticker and draw animals with blubber swimming in the cold water.

Beluga whale skin is 100 times thicker than human skin. And under *that* is another 4 to 10 inches of blubber!

Penguins have strong flippers for swimming. They can stay underwater for up to 20 minutes to catch food!

Some whales can have blubber almost 20 inches thick. That's wider then 2 basketballs put together!

coniferous forest!

Many animals in the coniferous forest **hibernate** for the winter. This means that when the weather is cold and there isn't much food available, they sleep to survive. Many months later, when the weather is warmer, they wake up!

To prepare to hibernate, animals eat extra food. Sticker and draw food for each animal.

Chipmunk

Bat

Chipmunks eat nuts, seeds, and fruit.

Bats eat insects.

Black Bear

Black bears eat roots, berries, insects, and even fish!

a walk in the forest

What does **coniferous** mean? Coniferous trees grow cones, and the cones hold seeds to grow more trees!

Cones come in all shapes and sizes! Sticker and draw cones on the trees.

Most coniferous trees are also **evergreen**—that means they are always green! They keep their needles all year long.

Animals like birds and squirrels break open cones to eat the seeds inside. Sticker and draw an animal opening a cone for seeds!

desert!

Sticker and draw a meal for each animal.

Tarantula

I eat insects, spiders, and small animals.

Meerkat

I eat insects, small animals, eggs, and plants. Even scorpions!

Rattlesnake

I eat small animals like mice and lizards.

Gila Monster

Gila monsters store fat and water in their large tails!

I eat insects, eggs, and small animals.

Camel

I eat grass and bushes.

Scorpion

I eat insects, spiders, and lizards.

Kangaroo

I eat grass, flowers, and leaves.

Scorpions can survive up to 12 months without food!

Armadillo

I eat insects, plants, fruit, and more.

my favorite animal

Sticker and draw yourself with your favorite animal.

Sticker and draw your other favorite animals.

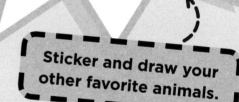

My favorite animal lives in _____.

A sound this animal might make is _____.

This animal eats _____.

The best thing about this animal is _____

_____.

rainforest!

Rainforests have the greatest **biodiversity** on Earth! That means rainforests have the greatest variety of plants and animals of all habitats.

Sticker and draw the different types of animals that live in the rainforest.

lives underground

is poisonous

Scientists believe half of all species on Earth live in the rainforest!

climbs trees

has sharp teeth

has a sticky tongue

hangs upside down

Rainforests can be found on all the continents except Antarctica.

high and low

Most rainforest animals live over 100 feet above the ground in the **canopy**, which is the upper parts of the trees. That's like living on top of a 10-story building! To move around the canopy, many animals jump, fly, or even glide!

Sticker and draw the animals that live in the canopy.

To study life in canopies, scientists build walkways high in the trees!

Animals cannot see very far through the leaves, vines, and branches. Many use loud cries or songs to communicate.